T0191333

THE SCIENCE BEHIND

UNICORNS, DRAGONS, AND KRAKEN

JOY LIN AND VIOLET TOBACCO

Gareth Stevens
PUBLISHING

Please visit our website,
www.garethstevens.com.
For a free color catalog of all
our high-quality books, call
toll free 1-800-542-2595 or
fax 1-877-542-2596.

Published in 2025 by
Gareth Stevens Publishing
2544 Clinton St.
Buffalo, NY 14224

First published in Great Britain in 2021 by Wayland
Text © Joy Lin, 2021
Artwork and design © Hodder and Stoughton, 2021

Editors: Elise Short and Grace Glendinning
Designer: Peter Scoulding
Illustration: Violet Tobacco

Cataloging-in-Publication Data

Names: Lin, Joy, author. | Tobacco, Violet, illustrator.
Title: The science behind unicorns, dragons, and kraken /
  by Joy Lin, illustrated by Violet Tobacco.
Description: New York : Gareth Stevens Publishing, 2025. |
  Series: Monster science | Includes glossary and index.
Identifiers: ISBN 9781538294260 (pbk.) | ISBN 9781538294277 (library bound) |
  ISBN 9781538294284 (ebook)
Subjects: LCSH: Animals, Mythical--Juvenile literature. | Mythology--Juvenile literature. |
  Folklore--Juvenile literature. | Science--Juvenile literature.
Classification: LCC GR825.L56 2025 | DDC 398'.4--dc23

Printed in the United States of America

CPSIA compliance information: Batch #CSGS25: For further information contact Gareth Stevens at 1-800-542-2595.

Find us on

CONTENTS

INTRODUCTION

Are you fascinated by weird and wonderful creatures? Have you ever wondered if the mythical creatures that live in all of your favorite stories — such as unicorns, dragons, and the kraken — could actually exist? Are you curious about how tales of these mysterious beasts first started?

Then you've come to the right place. This book is here to help. By setting out the science behind these mythical creatures, you'll find out whether there's a chance that they might exist now or might have existed in the past — and whether you'll ever have a chance of spotting one.

Meet the Monsters

We begin with unicorns. They've captured human imaginations around the world for centuries. In the 4th century BCE, a Greek doctor recorded tales he'd been told by travelers from India of a group of wild, white donkeys with purple heads, blue eyes, and 18-inch (46-cm) horns on their foreheads.

More recently, but still over 3,000 years ago, in China, the mythical one-horned qilin — with the hooves of a horse, the body of a deer, and the tail of an ox — is said to have made its first appearance in the garden of legendary emperor Huangdi. In images, the qilin looks quite fierce, but it was described as a gentle creature that appeared at important moments in Chinese history.

Images of unicorns reappeared later in the Middle Ages in European folklore, paintings, and tapestries. And of course today they frequently feature in children's stories as kindly creatures of magic and mystery.

But what about dragons? Many cultures around the world tell age-old dragon stories. The creatures they describe take many different forms, from Egypt's Akhekh with its snake-like body, four legs, and wings, to Scandinavia's Fafnir, with its armored scales that no ordinary weapon could penetrate; from European dragons that look like giant flying dinosaurs with wings, to Asian dragons that are more like giant snakes with feet, talons, and the ability to fly without wings. Still featured in popular culture today, often fire-breathing and usually able to fly, do dragons resemble any real creatures on Earth?

You may or may not have heard the name "kraken," but we all know tales of frighteningly large and angry sea monsters. Kraken sightings throughout history have been concentrated in the waters between Europe and North America. Reported glimpses of the creature date back as far as 1180 in the Norwegian Sea, which stretches from Norway to Greenland, and they're terrifying! The kraken is said to be squid- or octopus-like, and absolutely enormous. Over the years, the monster has fascinated scientists and novelists alike — could a massive sea monster perhaps exist in unexplored parts of our oceans?

What if these creatures were real? If we apply science to what makes these creatures unique, could they theoretically exist? How would flying unicorns' wings support their muscular bodies? How would dragons breathe fire? How much food would a kraken need to eat to fuel its gigantic body?

We'll answer these questions, but keep your eyes peeled at all times — you never know where a creature might be hiding!

Feeling brave? Let's get started...

Unicorns

What is it about unicorns that delights us so much? Except for the horn, of course, they share most of their characteristics with horses. Beautiful and majestic creatures, horses are amazing in many ways.

HORSE EVOLUTION?

If we think of a unicorn as a magical horse, with a spiraling horn on its forehead, that can do more or less everything a horse does, is it a creature that really could exist? How realistic would it be for a species of horse to evolve to develop a horn?

Let's Start with Some Horse Facts

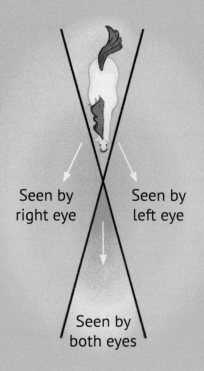

Seen by
right eye

Seen by
left eye

Seen by
both eyes

Horses have the largest eyes of any land mammal and, because their eyes are on the sides of their head, they can see nearly all around them — almost 360 degrees — at the same time! Horses are naturally excellent runners, reaching speeds of up to 55 miles (88 km) per hour — think of a car driving along comfortably in the slow lane of a highway. While humans take a long time — six months or more — to learn to crawl, a horse can get up and run within hours of being born. That is impressive! Did you know that a horse can also sleep standing up? And that a horse's teeth are so big, they take up more space in its head than its brain?

Darwin's Big Idea

Charles Darwin (1809–1882) worked out a theory of evolution that suggests a species develops through the "natural selection" of various traits it inherits from its ancestors. Those traits improve a creature's ability to compete, survive, and reproduce in a particular environment.

Here's an example: if most of the seeds available on an island are quite large, then the larger-beaked birds that live around the island would find it easier to eat them. That means they'd secure more food and stand a better chance of survival than small-beaked birds.

More big-beaked birds would survive long enough to have babies, passing more big-beaked genes (the set of instructions passed down by parents that determine traits such as eye color or beak size) down to the next generation.

If the process is repeated over generations without anything to disrupt it — such as a predator with a taste for big-beaked birds — eventually big-beaked birds will dominate the island.

HORN DILEMMA

So could a process of evolution create a unicorn horn on a horse? If so, could it be the sort of spiraling horn we see in pictures of unicorns?

We know plenty of mammals have two horns — sheep, cows, and goats, for example. Their horns are formed of bone and covered in a protein called keratin — the stuff our hair and fingernails are made from. Horses' hooves are also made of keratin, so a horse's body does have the ability to create the substance that forms a horn.

But what about the spiral? Well, that's possible too. We know there is already a natural process that helps shape the twisty horns of the spiral-horned antelope. There is a trait in an antelope's genes that controls their growth with growth spurts, or "growth pulses." The pulses make the horn grow faster and thinner some of the time and thicker and slower at others, helping create the corkscrew shape.

HORN USES

Now, if a horse did have a horn, what would it be used for? Horses are prey animals, so they are mostly built to avoid or escape attack. If they had no option but to fight for survival, however, having a pointy horn to stab at enemies could certainly be an advantage.

So if a mutation (the arrival of a new trait) occurred one day and a few horses developed a small horn, they might be able to use them to get out of sticky situations — perhaps without even having to fight! A predator might take one look at the horn and decide to chase some other (hornless) horse instead. With fewer hornless horses surviving, these horned genes would be passed down to the next generation, creating the first "pre-unicorns."

In later generations, the horns would become longer and longer ... but not too long. A huge horn would be too heavy to swing at a predator; it would slow the horse down and get in the way when lowering its head to eat.

MAGICAL HORN MYTH

Let's look into the idea that a unicorn horn itself has powers. In Europe, from the 10th to the 16th centuries, many legends described the magic of unicorn horns, from water purification to healing and protective properties. Royalty at the time collected "unicorn" horns because they were seen as very valuable. So is there any scientific evidence that a horn could do any of these miraculous things?

Well, let's remember what they are made of: keratin — the same material as our fingernails and hair. No miracle cures found in those! However, the horns were often narwhal tusks (see pages 13–14), made of ivory, which as it turns out doesn't have any magical properties either. It was a lack of scientific knowledge that made people believe that horns, among other odd animal parts, could help cure illnesses. Now that we know a lot more, science can tell us that, unfortunately, there's nothing magical about a horn.

WINGING IT

From horns ... to wings. Have you ever seen pictures of winged unicorns, sometimes called alicorns or pegacorns? These creatures look particularly stunning, but could an animal as large as a horse really get off the ground, even if it did have an impressive pair of wings?

Horses are built for running, and even though they're herbivores, they have a great metabolism that turns the grass and hay they eat into running muscles. A typical adult horse weighs about 1,540 to 2,200 pounds (700 to 1,000 kg), and that's *without* wings and a horn. Today, the largest flying bird by weight is the great bustard, and the largest great bustard only weighs about 44 pounds (20 kg). A horse is 35 to 50 times heavier!

Unthinkable Wingspan

Imagine the wing size it would take to support an alicorn! At 10 feet (3 m), the wandering albatross has the largest wingspan of any living bird. Yet, an albatross's wings support a maximum bodyweight of 10 pounds (4.5 kg).

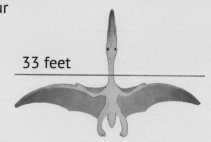

10 feet

Compare that to the largest pterosaur (a flying reptile from dinosaur times) that ever existed — the *Quetzalcoatlus*. This giant creature had a 33-foot (10-m) wingspan (about the length of a city bus). Even so, its wings only supported a bodyweight of about 440 pounds (200 kg) — roughly a quarter of the weight of an adult horse (without wings and a horn). Getting the alicorn off the ground would require wings much, much larger than the ones shown in picture books.

33 feet

Many, many feet

Hollow Bones?

Birds are specially designed for flight, right down to their skeletons. Unlike most animals, they have hollow bones that keep their bodies light. If winged unicorns are from the horse family, it's highly unlikely their bones would be hollow after thousands of years of evolution, as they also need to support their bodies on land!

Even more ... think about how cold your fingers get when the temperature drops. This is because they're farther away from your heart and have less blood pumping through them. A unicorn's heart couldn't pump blood far enough for its extremely long wings to function. Unless a unicorn's ancestor was a bird instead of a horse, it is very unlikely a unicorn would ever take off.

THE REAL UNICORNS

So you wouldn't ever see a flying unicorn, but what if we're happy to settle for a wingless unicorn?

"Unicorn" literally means "one horn," and although most animal horns come in pairs, there are a few creatures with just the one. Those Indian travelers who described seeing a unicorn in India (see page 5) could very well have spotted an Indian rhinoceros, which has just one horn.

UNICORN OF THE SEA

But the Indian rhinoceros's horn doesn't grow much longer than 40 inches (100 cm). If you want to see an animal with a beautiful long and twisted single horn, you'll need to dive underwater.

Growing to around 8 feet (2.4 m) in length, a narwhal's tusk is actually a tooth that grows out from the top of a male narwhal's skull. Scientists only discovered what the tusk is used for in 2014, when a study showed that nerve endings in the center of the tusk connect to the narwhal's brain, passing information about water temperature and chemical changes in the environment. This means, they concluded, that the tusk probably helps the narwhal to find food or a mate. Some video footage also shows narwhals using their tusk to bash unsuspecting fish, stunning them before they snap them up for supper.

Not My Horn!

People once used narwhal tusks as proof that unicorns really existed, so seeing a narwhal may be the closest you'll ever get to meeting a storybook unicorn. To spot a narwhal you'll need to head toward the Arctic, where they usually swim in groups of 15 to 20. If you're incredibly lucky, you might see a group of 100 or even 1,000 narwhals swimming together! And that might be even more exciting than spotting a mythical unicorn.

Probability of ever meeting a unicorn:
LOW

Dragons

Dragons have been described in all sorts of shapes and sizes, depending on where in the world their legend began. In this chapter we'll focus on the fire-breathing, wing-flying sort that are popular in Western culture. Is the fire breathing actually possible? And, if so, how on earth could it happen? Also, if it's impossible for a horse to get off the ground (see pages 11–12), what chance is there that a dragon could ever fly?

A Burning Question

Let's start with the fire breathing. How does a fire start in the first place?

Before anything can burn, three essential elements need to be present: heat, fuel, and oxygen. If one of these is missing, the fire won't happen.

Rub two sticks together to make a fire and you create friction. It's this friction that creates the heat.

Vapors produced by the heat react speedily with the oxygen in the nearby air, causing gas to be released that heats the fuel (the material that burns, in this case: wood) further and eventually causes it to catch fire.

The burning fuel releases more vapors that react with the oxygen, the cycle continues, and the fire gets hotter. This is called a chain reaction, and it is often drawn as a fire tetrahedron, as shown (right).

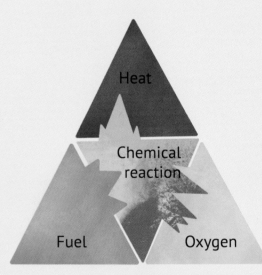

Heat

Chemical reaction

Fuel

Oxygen

The more oxygen there is, the hotter the fire will be. Low-oxygen fire is yellow, and high-oxygen fire is blue. So when you look at a flame, you can see which is the hottest part.

When one of the three elements — oxygen, fuel, or heat — goes, the fire dies. For example, a fire blanket can put out a small fire because it smothers the flames and stops any more oxygen from getting to the fire.

Even Hotter

Hot

Fire in the Belly

Now, if a dragon was going to breathe fire, it would need to store fuel in its body, then find a way to ignite that fuel. You're probably thinking that sounds impossible, but it isn't, necessarily.

Scientists have identified a creature that really does have inbuilt fuel tanks, though it's a bit smaller than your average dragon. The 1-inch-long (2.5-cm) bombardier beetle stores the chemicals hydrogen peroxide and hydroquinone in two separate chambers in its belly. When it feels threatened, the crafty beetle mixes these two ingredients together and creates a chemical reaction that releases heat. The result? A boiling hot spray shoots toward its attacker!

So maybe a dragon could store chemicals to burn as fuel in its body too?

Creating flames

The question is, suppose a dragon did carry the fuel in its body, how would it create flames? There are a couple of options. The fire might start chemically: there are many combinations of chemicals that react, when mixed together, to create heat hot enough to start a flame without even needing a spark.

Then again, the fire could be started mechanically. When friction and impact are added to flammable materials, a spark can be created to ignite the fuel. Even if the dragon doesn't have the materials in its body to start a spark, it could chew together flint rocks or bits of steel to create an impact that would produce the necessary spark. So breathing fire really might be possible!

Up, Up, and Away ...

So that's the fire breathing figured out. What about the flying?
Let's take a look at how flying usually works:

Gravity is the force that pulls people and things toward Earth.
In order to get a plane (or a dragon) off the ground, a greater force
is needed to act against gravity. Generally, the more an object or
animal weighs, the more energy it takes to fly.

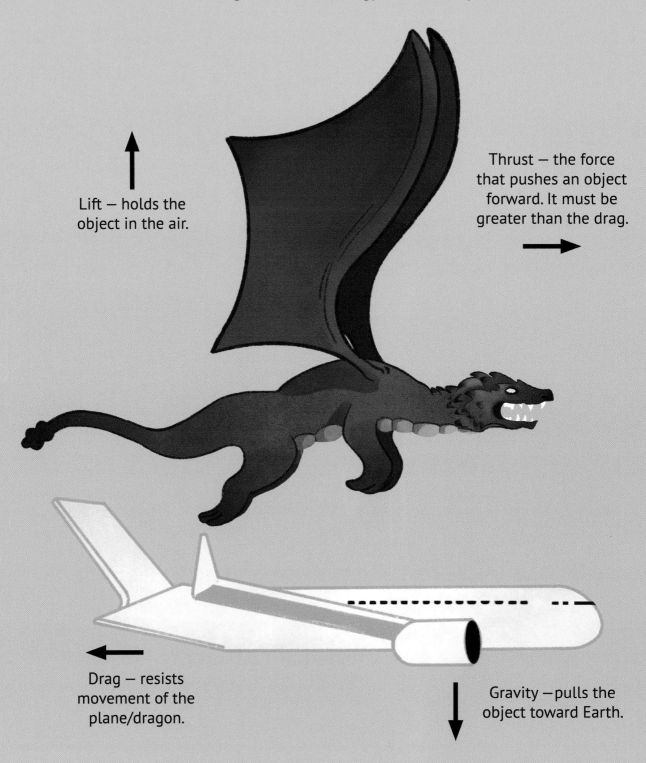

Lift — holds the
object in the air.

Thrust — the force
that pushes an object
forward. It must be
greater than the drag.

Drag — resists
movement of the
plane/dragon.

Gravity —pulls the
object toward Earth.

Cliffjumper

Of course, flight doesn't always require lift-off. Even if an animal can't work up enough force to fly straight up from the ground, it can still achieve flight by either getting a running start to create some speed or by jumping from a great height and catching the air to glide for a while.

Even humans can glide through the air this way — you might have seen videos of people wearing wingsuits and jumping off cliffs. Yikes! It's very, very dangerous, and you shouldn't try this yourself. These carefully designed suits enable human flight — to a point. The shape of the suit creates lift, decreasing the pull of gravity so that the wearer falls to Earth more slowly, but still not slowly enough for a safe landing: wingsuits also need a built-in parachute.

So perhaps a dragon could glide for limited distances like this, rather than fly. Gliding doesn't need much wing movement, so it would use less energy. But would the dragon have the same trouble landing as we humans do?

FULL OF HOT AIR

What if a dragon took to the skies like a hot-air balloon does, using only different air temperatures? You might find this hard to believe, but even though you can't see it, air isn't empty. It's full of all sorts of different molecules, including hydrogen, oxygen, and carbon. These elements all have mass (weightiness), therefore air has mass too.

The reason hot-air balloons can take to the sky is that hot air weighs less than normal air, so the weight of the hot-air balloon is *less* than the amount of air it pushes aside. This is called buoyancy, the same way a boat can float by pushing aside the same weight of water as the boat and its contents.

Of course, the difference between hot air and normal air is not huge, so the hot-air balloon itself needs to be enormous (with an awful lot of hot air inside it), and the basket it carries beneath it needs to be tiny and light in order to get off the ground.

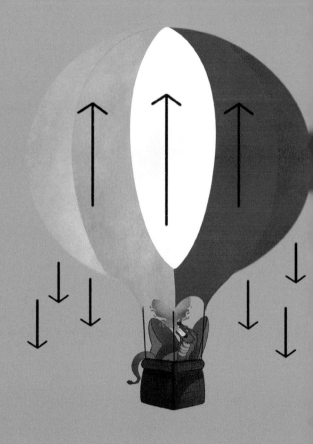

With these scientific facts in mind, do you think a dragon could create enough hot air in its body to turn itself into a giant hot-air balloon, generating enough lifting force to help it take off? It may just be possible, under some very particular circumstances.

First, the dragon would have to have a belly that could expand, much like the way a toad can expand itself. (Common toads can send air to different parts of their bodies to make themselves look too big for a predator to eat.) Next, as long as the dragon could control the hot air in the same way hot air in a balloon is controlled — adding more air to fly higher and releasing it carefully to sink down again — the landing problem would also be solved.

Dragon Dinners

One last thing: we may not know the size of a Western dragon for certain, but we do know most people think of them as seriously large. So how much food would dragons need to eat in order to fuel themselves for flight? Well, lucky for us, scientists have already done this calculation, and they figure dragons would need approximately 120,000 calories to fuel just one hour of flight (about 60 times what an adult human needs in one day). Considering there are only about 500 calories in 16 ounces (450 g) of meat, a dragon would need to eat a pretty big animal just to keep itself in the air for that one hour.

Let's say dragons stick to cattle for lunch instead of humans (phew!), the odds are there's nowhere on Earth that could provide enough cattle to feed even a single active dragon, let alone a family of dragons.

In short, we should probably assume big flying dragons don't exist. If they did, and if they ate whatever or whomever they wanted whenever they needed the energy, they'd have made a lot of the larger species on Earth extinct by now. And if they couldn't find enough food to feed themselves, then they'd have become extinct too!

Probability of ever meeting an enormous fire-breathing dragon: LOW

(but it might just be possible to find a tiny one.)

Kraken

The mention of a kraken once spread fear among all sailors.

This giant sea monster was described by some as being the size of a small island, with enormous arms that could flip a ship. Sometimes the kraken was said to swim in circles around a ship, creating a whirlpool to suck it underwater. After that, the monster got straight to work swallowing the crew whole. No wonder the sailors were scared!

But were these stories true? Could a creature so vast really exist, and could you ever see one? Or were they just sailors' tales to terrify mindless landlubbers?

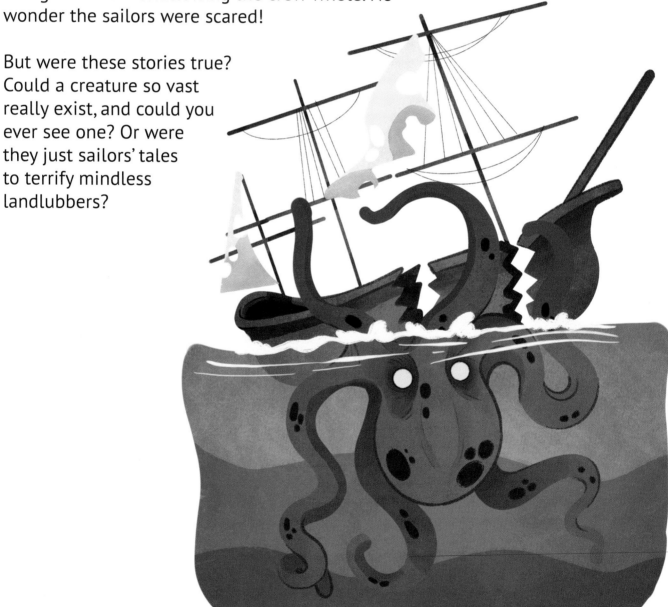

Hooks and Suckers

First, let's try to identify this creature's potential species. The idea of a giant creature prowling below the surface of the water, waiting to attack unsuspecting ships, isn't too hard to imagine. With its enormous arms, would the kraken belong to the squid or the octopus family? Both are cephalopods with long bodies, eight arms, and the ability to regenerate (which basically means that if a squid or octopus loses an arm, or another part of its body, it can grow a replacement)!

Appearance-wise, an octopus has a round head, while a squid's head is triangular. Each octopus arm has one or two rows of suckers, while a squid's arms can have hooks, suckers, or sucker rings. A squid also has two fins on its head and two extra-long tentacles.

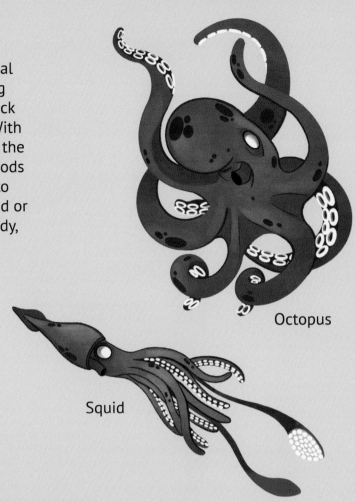

Octopus

Squid

Giant or Colossal?

In historic paintings and etchings of kraken, they seem to look more like an octopus, but in terms of size they're more similar to squid, mainly because squid can sometimes grow to be absolutely massive (longest found so far was about 60 feet [18 m] long)!

There are, in fact, two types of massive squid: the giant squid and the colossal squid. The first is the longest and the second is the heaviest of all squid. The giant squid is found in every ocean on Earth, and the other lives in the Antarctic Ocean. It's more likely that the giant squid is the basis for kraken legends since it is easier to stumble upon.

SQUIDTASTIC

Even when they aren't huge, squid are fascinating creatures.

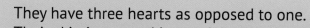

- They have three hearts as opposed to one.
- Their skin is covered in special cells called chromatophores that allow them to change color, so they can hide from predators by blending in with their surroundings.
- If that doesn't trick attackers, most squid are able to shoot black ink in defense. Some species have ink sacs filled with colorful, glowing bioluminescent mucus (a bit like the ink in a highlighter pen). The squirting ink protects them by blinding and confusing a would-be attacker, giving the squid a chance to get away.
- Some deep-water squid have glow-in-the-dark organs to help them navigate in the deep, dark waters they inhabit!
- There's one type of little flying squid that can travel nearly 100 feet (30 m) through the air — in just three seconds (wow!) — to avoid a predator.

Luckily, there have been no reports of really big squid being able to fly. That really would be scary!

SQUIDZILLA

So where does the kraken come into this? Scandinavian legends and folklore report that the kraken was as big as an island or a mountain. Well, when you compare these stories to the largest members of the squid family ... fact and fiction don't quite add up.

The biggest squid ever recorded was a whopping 60 feet (18 m) long and weighed about 1,985 pounds (900 kg). Imagine 10 tall adults standing on top of each other's heads to get an idea of how big and heavy she was! And we can be confident this was a female squid because the females of the species are about twice the size of the males.

Let's compare this to the size of the average ship in the year 1180, when the first kraken sighting was recorded. The most common ship at the time was about 55 feet (17 m) long. So even our regular old giant squid must have been a terrifying sight, floating alongside a ship!

Still ... that's no mountain.

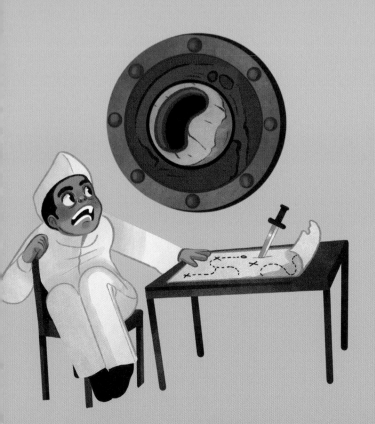

EYEBALL TO EYEBALL

Maybe the exaggerated size reports came from a sailor making eye contact with a giant squid. At 10 inches (25 cm), the squid's eye alone would have been the size of a basketball. Giant squid have the largest eyes of any creature in the animal kingdom because, as they spend most of their time lurking in the deepest, darkest waters of the ocean, their eyes need to absorb as much light as possible to help them spot predators and prey. Making eye contact with an eye that big is sure to give you nightmares … and you'd be forgiven for imagining the body attached to it might be the size of a mountain!

A SHY CREATURE

Despite its size, the giant squid seems to be quite a shy creature. Dwelling near the bottom of the ocean — between 1,640 and 3,280 feet (500–1,000 m) down — it's more often seen dead than alive, when it has floated up from the depths. For a long time, the remains of a detached arm or tentacle, or a dead squid washing up on shore, was the only evidence people had that the creatures really existed.

The first video recording of a live giant squid didn't happen until 2006, and it wasn't filmed in its own habitat until 2012! So it seems quite unlikely that it would willingly come to the surface to attack ships. Those dead bits of body probably did help fuel stories about the kraken, though.

Tentacles Galore

The big squid might be shy, but it's no gentle giant. Hiding in the dark is helpful when it comes to hunting prey, especially if you've got tentacles. And a giant squid's tentacles are impressive. It attacks horizontally by stretching out its tentacles in front of it. Twice the length of its body, they can shoot out across a distance of more than 33 feet (10 m).

Once the squid has caught something, its tentacles wrap around the prey in a similar way to how a python rapidly envelops its prey within coils of its body. The tentacles then feed the prey through thousands more 2-inch-wide (5-cm) suckers along its arms and up to its beak, where the poor victim is gradually chopped to pieces and eaten. Death by giant squid must be seriously nasty. A squid even has teeth on its tongue (also known as a radula)!

Sailor for Dinner?

There is no doubt the fierce giant squid could pose a serious threat to any human diver it saw as prey. To add to this, as we saw with the dragons on page 21, it takes a huge amount of calories to sustain a gigantic animal's daily activities.

When it comes to food for sea monsters there's lots of space to roam in search of prey — literally plenty of fish in the sea. A blue whale, for example, manages to eat up to 4.5 tons (4 mt) of krill (small shrimplike creatures) every day. That's the weight of two small cars!

On the other hand, it's easy to see why kraken would want to eat sailors — they'd be highly nutritious! Humans are a great source of protein and fat. However, there is the small issue of the boat that stands between a sailor and the unforgiving sea ...

A THREAT TO SHIPS?

As we've seen, the giant squid is an effective and formidable predator. But could it take down a ship?

There are lots of reports throughout history of giant squid attacking ships. One account as recent as 2003 reports that a giant squid 23 to 26 feet (7 to 8 m) long had clamped on to the hull of a French racing yacht off the Portuguese island of Madeira. Two of the tentacles were blocking the rudder, which steers the ship. But unlike most stories featuring the kraken, the crew did not have to fight off the creature in a ferocious battle. The squid released its grip when they stopped the boat. It seems unlikely that its goal was to sink the boat or that it even had the force to do so.

MONSTER MUNCHER

It certainly seems possible that a kraken-like giant squid could survive in the ocean, lurking in depths that humans hardly visit, at a size much bigger than any we've seen so far. Huge sea creatures do exist — blue whales can measure up to 92 feet (28 m) long, but as they only eat small sea creatures, they aren't much of a threat to humans.

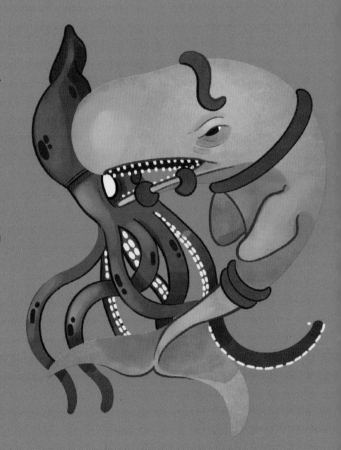

The sperm whale doesn't attack humans either, but it does go for giant squid. While they grow to just 57 feet (17.5 m) in length, sperm whales can weigh up to 50 tons (45 mt)! But how do we know a sperm whale has ever *won* a fight with a giant squid? Because bits of giant squid have been found in the stomachs of sperm whales.

We also know that giant squid don't go down without a fight because of the large, round wounds inflicted on a sperm whale's skin by the serrated rings on a giant squid's suckers. It's thought giant squid are so important to a sperm whale's diet, that if they were to become extinct, the sperm whale population would suffer massively too.

We know less about the oceans on our own planet than we do about our solar system. So much about the ocean is mysterious. It is dark, vast, deep, and unpredictable. So, it's possible that a squid-like creature could grow to the size of the mythological kraken ... but it's unlikely you'll ever see one!

Probability of ever meeting a vicious kraken: LOW

Even so, if you happen to be a sailor, watch out!

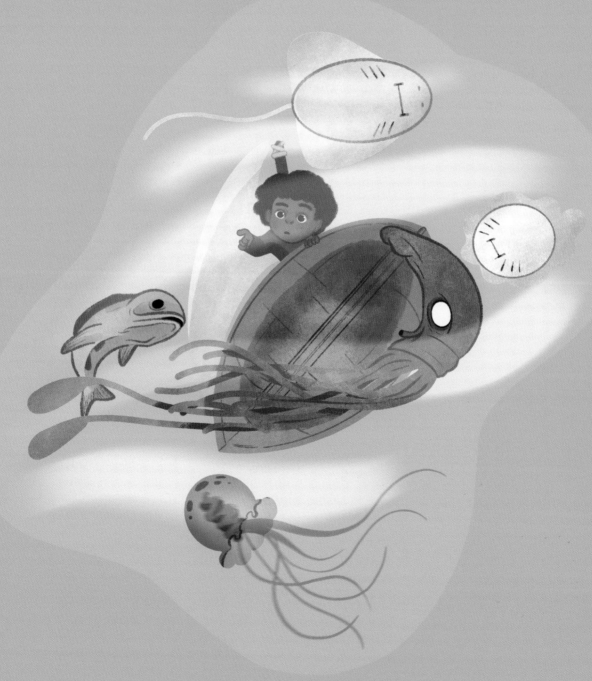

GLOSSARY

absorb to take something in or soak it up

ancestor a person from several generations before to whom another person is related

bioluminescent describing an organism that gives off light

buoyancy the ability to float in water or another fluid

cephalopods predatory creatures in the mollusk family, such as squid

chain reaction a process in which the active products themselves increase or spread the reaction

characteristics features of a person, place, or thing that help identify them

chemical reaction a process that changes the molecules or ions in a substance

chromatophores cells or other small structures that contain the natural coloring of an animal or plant

dominate be the most important or obvious thing in a time and/or place

elements things that make up matter and can't be broken down into simpler substances

evidence the information that shows if an idea is true or not

evolve to change and develop over a period of time

flammable easily set on fire

force an effect that changes the motion of an object

formidable causing fear by being large, powerful, or skilled

friction the resistance that a surface has when moving against another surface

generating producing or creating something

ignite to catch fire or cause to catch fire

inherits genetically receives a feature from an ancestor

ivory a hard, white material that makes up the tusks of several animals, including elephants and narwhals

landlubber a person who is not familiar with the sea or sailing

legend a very old and well-known story that may or may not be true

majestic having impressive beauty or size

mass in physics, the amount of physical matter belonging to an object

metabolism the chemical changes in the cells of living things that produces energy to maintain life

molecules groups of atoms connected together

mucus a slimy substance put out by some plants and animals, often for protection

mythical describing something made up in the past to explain religious beliefs or customs

nerve endings thin branches at the end of a nerve cell, used to make contact with another cell

nutritious describing food that is nourishing and effective for staying healthy

penetrate to go into or through something

proportion the relationship of one thing to another in terms of amount, size, or number

purification taking out dangerous or dirty substances that have contaminated something else

radula a structure of tiny teeth in a mollusk, used for scraping food off a surface

regenerate to grow new tissue after it is lost or damaged

reproduce to create offspring

Scandinavian relating to people or things from countries that include Norway, Sweden, and Denmark

serrated having a jagged edge

smothers puts out a fire by covering it

species a group of plants or animals that share the same main characteristics and are able to breed with each other

tapestries pieces of fabric that have pictures or designs woven or embroidered on them

tentacles thin, flexible limbs on an animal

tetrahedron a triangular pyramid

theoretically according to an idea, rather than experience or practice

theory an idea used to explain a situation or an action taken

vapors substances floating in the air

FURTHER INFORMATION

Further freaky science reading:

Cause, Effect and Chaos! In the Animal Kingdom
by Paul Mason
(Wayland, 2020)

A Question of Science: Why Can't Penguins Fly?
And Other Questions About Animals
by Anna Claybourne
(Wayland, 2020)

The *Body Bits* series, including the following
fantastic books:
Astounding Animal Body Facts
Dead-Awesome Dinosaur Body Facts
Eye-Popping Plant Part Facts
Hair-Raising Human Body Facts
by Paul Mason
(Gareth Stevens, 2023)

Animals in Disguise
by Michael Bright
(Wayland, 2020)

Places to see freaky science up close:

American Museum of Natural History
200 Central Park West
New York, NY 10024
https://www.amnh.org

National Museum of Natural History
10th Street and Constitution Avenue NW
Washington, DC 20560
https:/naturalhistory.si.edu

Natural History Museum
900 Exposition Boulevard
Los Angeles, CA 90007
https://nhm.org

Canada Museum of Nature
240 McLeod Street
Ottawa, ON K2P 2R1
https://nature.ca/en/

INDEX